TIME

Visions of the
'60s

John F. Kennedy and Friends
PAUL SCHUTZER • *Baltimore* • *September 1960*

TIME

MANAGING EDITOR Richard Stengel
ART DIRECTOR D.W. Pine

Visions of the '60s
The Images That Define the Decade

EDITOR Kelly Knauer
DESIGNER Ellen Fanning
PICTURE EDITOR Patricia Cadley
WRITING AND RESEARCH Tresa McBee
COPY EDITOR Bruce Christopher Carr

TIME HOME ENTERTAINMENT

PUBLISHER Richard Fraiman
GENERAL MANAGER Steven Sandonato
EXECUTIVE DIRECTOR, MARKETING SERVICES Carol Pittard
DIRECTOR, RETAIL AND SPECIAL SALES Tom Mifsud
DIRECTOR, NEW PRODUCT DEVELOPMENT Peter Harper
DIRECTOR, BOOKAZINE DEVELOPMENT AND MARKETING Laura Adam
PUBLISHING DIRECTOR, BRAND MARKETING Joy Butts
ASSISTANT GENERAL COUNSEL Helen Wan
BOOK PRODUCTION MANAGER Suzanne Janso
DESIGN AND PREPRESS MANAGER Anne-Michelle Gallero
BRAND MANAGER Michela Wilde
ASSOCIATE PREPRESS MANAGER Alex Voznesenskiy

SPECIAL THANKS
Christine Austin, Jeremy Biloon, Glenn Buonocore, Jim Childs, Susan Chodakiewicz, Rose Cirrincione, Brian Fellows, Jacqueline Fitzgerald, Carrie Frazier, Lauren Hall, Malena Jones, Brynn Joyce, Mona Li, Robert Marasco, Amy Migliaccio, Kimberly Posa, Brooke Reger, Dave Rozzelle, Al Rufino, Ilene Schreider, Adriana Tierno, TIME Imaging, Sydney Webber

We welcome your comments and suggestions about TIME Books. Please write to us at:
TIME Books, Attention: Book Editors, P.O. Box 11016, Des Moines, IA 50336-1016

To order any of our hardcover Collector's Edition books, please call us at 1-800-327-6388.
Monday–Friday, 7 a.m.–8 p.m., or Saturday, 7 a.m.–6 p.m., Central Time.

ISBN 10: 1-60320-110-6
ISBN 13: 978-1-60320-110-0
Library of Congress Control Number: 2010927623

To enjoy TIME's frequently updated coverage of today's news, visit: **time.com**

Unknown soldier *Veteran combat photographer Horst Faas didn't get this young American's name when he took his picture in Vietnam on June 18, 1965; the soldier let his helmet do the talking*

Contents

GAB ARCHIVE—REDFERNS—GETTY IMAGES (11)

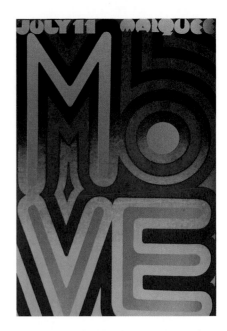

Rock Concert Poster Art

VARIOUS ARTISTS
San Francisco • 1966-70

How to capture the explosive power of rock music in a two-dimensional poster? San Francisco artists used a toolbox of psychedelic effects to get the job done: elaborate typefaces and malleable lettering, screaming Day-Glo colors, a dash of Op Art tromp l'oeil, a hint of sex and skin. The results captured the energy and innocence of an era when new music and new drugs seemed capable of changing the world.

Faces *of the 1960s*

Muhammad Ali Works Out

THOMAS HOEPKER
London • 1966

Muhammad Ali was more than a great face of the '60s: he was a great mouth of the '60s. When he rose to fame at the Rome Olympics in 1960, the young heavyweight from Louisville, Ky., was known by his birth name, Cassius Clay, and he delighted Americans with his put-on braggadocio and clever rhymes celebrating his own prowess ("Who would have thought/ When they came to the fight/ That they'd witness the launching/ Of a human satellite?"). But the champ's carefree cool changed over the decade: Clay became a committed Black Muslim, perplexing many fans, then lost more of them when he refused to serve in the military during the Vietnam War. Yet he never lost his way with a phrase; he defended his antiwar stance with the memorable quote "I ain't got no quarrel with them Viet Cong."

John and Caroline Kennedy Visit Their Father's Office

CECIL STOUGHTON
Washington • October 1963

At 43, John F. Kennedy was the youngest President to take office since Theodore Roosevelt in 1901. Like Roosevelt, Kennedy had young children whose antics captivated the nation. Above, daughter Caroline, 5, and son John Jr., 2, cavort in the Oval Office for their beaming father. The 1961 transition from aging World War II hero Dwight D. Eisenhower to the vigorous young Kennedy heralded a recurring theme of the decade: the struggle between youth and age.

Senator Kennedy Runs For the Presidency

PAUL SCHUTZER
Massachusetts • July 22, 1960

The convertible, the pillbox hat: the details of this picture immediately call to mind the 1963 assassination of President Kennedy in Dallas. But everyone was smiling in Massachusetts in July 1960, when Senator Kennedy returned from the Democratic National Convention in Los Angeles as the party's presidential candidate. When Mrs. Kennedy became First Lady in January 1961 and began her acclaimed renovation of the White House, she was only 31 years old.

The Beatles' First U.S. Appearance
UNKNOWN PHOTOGRAPHER
New York City • Feb. 9, 1964

If you saw it, you'll never forget it: the Beatles simply overwhelmed Americans with their talent and charm (and haircuts) when they appeared on Ed Sullivan's popular TV show less than three months after President Kennedy's assassination, providing the nation with a welcome blast of fun and energy. When reporters at their first press conference asked the cheeky Brits to sing a song, John Lennon set them straight: "We need money first."

Bob Dylan's First Recording Session
FRANK DRIGGS
New York City • November 1961

In the tradition of American self-invention, Robert Zimmerman dubbed himself Bob Dylan when he hung out his shingle as a musician. From the get-go, the disciple of Woody Guthrie was a master of the put-on. He told reporters yarns about his days riding freight trains out West, which they printed as truth. In reality, he had been living in a Jewish fraternity house at the University of Minnesota only a year before this photo was taken.

Ben Hogan and Arnold Palmer

UNKNOWN PHOTOGRAPHER
Augusta, Ga. • April 7, 1966

Two of golf's greatest legends shared a tee and a smoke at the 1966 Masters
Tournament. Hogan, then 53, retired from the game in 1971. Palmer, 36 in 1966,
was golf's most exciting and charismatic star in the 1960s, and he led the
charge to make the sport appealing to a wider and younger generation of fans,
a.k.a. "Arnie's Army." He won the Masters four times and helped make the
British Open a mandatory tournament for America's best professional players.

Peggy Fleming at the Winter Olympics

JOHN G. ZIMMERMAN
Grenoble, France • Feb. 5, 1968

The Californian, not yet 20, thrilled Americans by winning the nation's only gold medal at the 1968 Winter Games. Although adept at compulsory figures, Fleming was an artist whose lyrical style and fresh-faced good looks won fans of all ages. A straight arrow, the skater declared showboating footballer Joe Namath a "mess"—until, TIME reported, she was a guest on his TV show in 1969 and "melted like an icicle." A smitten Joe asked her for a date on camera.

Martin Luther King Jr. at the March on Washington

UNKNOWN PHOTOGRAPHER
Washington • Aug. 28, 1963

The civil rights leader's gift for oratory reached a peak with his memorable "I Have a Dream" speech to some 300,000 people at the March on Washington. Earlier in 1963, King had been jailed in Birmingham, Ala., for leading protests in which authorities used fire hoses and police dogs against nonviolent marchers, shocking the nation.

At year's end TIME named King Man of the Year for his leadership of the burgeoning movement for black civil rights and pointed out the cost of that role: "He himself has been stabbed in the chest, and physically attacked three more times; his home has been bombed three times, and he has been pitched into jail 14 times. His mail brings him a daily dosage of opinion in which he is by turn vilified and glorified. One letter says: 'This isn't a threat but a promise—your head will be blown off as sure as Christ made green apples.'"

AFP—GETTY IMAGES

**Alfred Hitchock Directs
Cast of *The Birds***

UNKNOWN PHOTOGRAPHER
Bodega Bay, Calif. • 1962

Hitchcock began working in the movies in 1921 in Britain, and the portly auteur
was at the top of his game in the early 1960s, riding the success of his famed
shocker *Psycho* (1960). Its follow-up, *The Birds* (1963), was a departure for him,
as the element of menace, essential to all his films, came from the natural world.

Peter O'Toole at a Costume Fitting

MARK KAUFFMAN

On location in Jordan, Spain or Morocco • 1961

O'Toole was a newcomer to U.S. audiences and not well known in Britain when he starred as the title character in David Lean's magnificent epic *Lawrence of Arabia* (1962), but his commanding performance and dreamy blue eyes lofted him into a memorable career. Below, costumers compare his *kaffiyeh* with the one in a photo of T.E. Lawrence.

U.S. Astronaut John Glenn

RALPH MORSE
Cape Canaveral, Fla. • 1961

When Glenn posed for this portrait, he was one of the seven men chosen
to be America's first astronauts, as the nascent National Aeronautics and
Space Administration strove to keep up with the alarming Soviet lead in
the space race. The fledgling Mercury program was plagued by rocket woes
early on, but on Feb. 20, 1962, Glenn became the first American to orbit the
earth—10 months after Russian cosmonaut Yuri Gagarin's historic flight.

Adolf Eichmann on Trial in Israel
UNKNOWN PHOTOGRAPHER
Jerusalem • June 22, 1961

The wounds of World War II still seemed fresh in the early 1960s, and never more so than when Adolf Eichmann, one of the architects of the Holocaust, was nabbed by Israeli Nazi-hunters in Argentina and put on trial in Jerusalem. Eichmann was kept in a protective glass box during the proceedings; his mild appearance and demeanor led political philosopher Hannah Arendt to coin the phrase "the banality of evil." Found guilty, he was executed in 1962.

Jimi Hendrix Sets Fire To His Guitar

ED CARAEFF
Monterey, Calif. • June 18, 1967

Just as the Beatles honed their chops in Hamburg, Germany, before returning to conquer Britain, U.S. guitar virtuoso Hendrix turned heads in London before returning to conquer the States. His guitar-burning stunt at the 1967 Monterey Pop Festival, his break-out performance, might have been a mere exercise in stagecraft if Hendrix hadn't had the talent to back up his antics—but he did.

Janis Joplin Sets Fire To Her Vocal Cords

ELLIOTT LANDY
New York City • Feb. 17, 1968

Joplin drank hard, sang hard, lived fast and died young—as did fellow rock superstar Hendrix. (Both musicians died at age 27 in 1970.) Joplin, born in Port Arthur, Texas, started out as a folksinging soprano but soon matured into a bluesy belter with a big voice. Above, she performs with Big Brother & the Holding Company, with the psyche-delic Joshua Light Show as stage décor.

Helen Gurley Brown at Work

SANTI VISALLI
New York City • circa 1965

The Arkansas-born Brown survived a tough childhood—her father died in an elevator accident and her family fought poverty—to become one of the nation's top female advertising copywriters. After her primer, *Sex and the Single Girl,* became a best seller in 1962, she was named editor of the struggling women's magazine *Cosmopolitan* in 1965. Brown turned it into a success by making it, well, Gurley-er: the magazine was in the vanguard of the era's sexual revolution. She told would-be "*Cosmo* Girls" that they could have it all— love, sex and money—and she was said to have claimed she wanted *Cosmo*'s voice to sound like young single women dishing dirt in office rest rooms.

Gloria Steinem at Home

AP PHOTOGRAPHER
New York City • March 18, 1970

The publication of Betty Friedan's 1963 best seller, *The Feminine Mystique,*
encouraged U.S. women to challenge their traditional roles, which many
increasingly viewed as restricting and unfair. One leader of the movement
was journalist Steinem, who opened eyes by working for a stint as a Bunny
in a Playboy Club in 1963, then writing about her experience for *Show*
magazine. After reporting for the groundbreaking city magazine *New York,*
Steinem emerged as a leading voice in the battle for women's rights. Her
1969 article "After Black Power, Women's Liberation" was an accurate fore-
cast, and she helped lead the movement by founding *Ms.* magazine in 1972.

Joe Namath After Super Bowl III

WALTER IOOSS JR.
Miami • Jan. 12, 1969

The 1960s bred a new sort of athlete: the bragging, swaggering star. Muhammad Ali kicked off the trend, and one worthy successor was New York Jets quarterback Namath, a.k.a. "Broadway Joe." When the Jets of the upstart American Football League were set to appear in Super Bowl III against the lordly Baltimore Colts of the venerable National Football League, Namath brashly "guaranteed" a Jets victory and was branded a showboat. Then he went out and beat the Colts, 16-7. End of story.

Mickey Mantle

UNKNOWN PHOTOGRAPHER
New York City • 1961

Handsome and cocky, Mantle first stepped into the huge shoes of Joe DiMaggio for the Yankee dynasty in the 1950s. But he was up to the challenge: the switch-hitter was a hard out for pitchers and was just as likely to run out a well-placed bunt as to smack a towering home run. In 1961 he and fellow Yankee Roger Maris put on a thrilling two-man show as they chased Babe Ruth's 1927 record of 60 home runs in a season. Maris finally hit 61, thanks to playing in eight more games than the Babe did.

Faces

Lyndon B. Johnson in Texas

YOICHI OKAMOTO
Stonewall, Texas • Nov. 20, 1965

Every President seems to agree with Harry Truman in describing the White House
as a "jail," and Johnson was no exception. He escaped as often as possible to his
expansive LBJ Ranch along the Pedernales River outside Stonewall, Texas, where his
personality seemed to expand in turn. Above, he wrangles a calf that seems as balky
as a Congressman. On one such visit, TIME's longtime White House correspondent
Hugh Sidey joined LBJ as the President, drinking beer from a paper cup, drove his
Lincoln Continental on a bumpy thrill-ride along the spread's dirt roads at 90 m.p.h.
When Sidey reported on the ride, he and the magazine tasted Johnson's famous wrath.

20

YOICHI OKAMOTO—LYNDON B. JOHNSON LIBRARY

Richard Nixon Campaigns for the Presidency

UNKNOWN PHOTOGRAPHER
Santa Barbara, Calif. • Sept. 17, 1968

Talk about a makeover: Nixon came back from the political grave in 1968, carefully distancing himself from the glowering figure who had declared to reporters after a failed run for Governor of California in 1962: "You won't have Dick Nixon to kick around anymore." With the nation reeling from the assassinations of Martin Luther King Jr. and Robert F. Kennedy, urban riots and the debacle of the Democratic Convention in Chicago, Nixon's call for "law and order" was welcome. He told aides that he loved appropriating the peace sign used by antiwar protesters. "It drives them crazy," he crowed.

Mick Jagger Fronts the Rolling Stones

BARON WOLMAN
Oakland, Calif. • Nov. 9, 1969

When the Rolling Stones first topped the charts during pop music's British Invasion of the mid-'60s, they positioned themselves as the dangerous alternative to the cute Beatles. Above, front man Jagger dons an Uncle Sam hat during the Stones' 1969 U.S. tour, which ended in disaster when Hell's Angels gang members, tasked with keeping order, ran amuck and a fan was stabbed to death at the Altamont Festival outside San Francisco in the decade's last month.

Elvis Presley's Comeback TV Special

UNKNOWN PHOTOGRAPHER
Burbank, Calif. • June 27, 1968

"What's that whatsit wriggling down the midway: that long damp thing with
the pale-green skin and the pollywog eyes and the squirmy little mouth?"
inquired TIME's film critic of the 1964 movie *Roustabout*. The answer, sadly,
was Presley, whose brilliance was buried for much of the '60s, when he gave
up performing live to star in a series of ever drearier, second-rate films. But
Elvis came back in style with this special, putting on his leathers and joining
his original backup musicians to play his old hits with all his sexy swagger.

Hugh Hefner and Associates At a Playboy Club

SLIM AARONS
Chicago • 1965

Hefner launched *Playboy* magazine in 1953, but the prophet of sexual liberation came into his own during the 1960s. As circulation soared, Hefner extended his brand by opening a series of Playboy Clubs around the country, where the servers—bosomy, scantily clad Bunnies—were the main draw.

Twiggy Models a Minidress

JOHN S. CLARKE
London • 1967

Here's Lesley Hornby, doing what she did best: look skinny in a mini. The 91-lb. British waif with big eyes, massive mascara, flat chest, bobbed hair and slim stems became the face of mod Britain at only 16. The daring miniskirt, championed by Britain's Mary Quant, became the signature look of the era.

Lee Harvey Oswald
Poses with Rifle

MARINA OSWALD
Dallas • circa late March 1963

Oswald grew up scrambling; by age 18 he had
lived in 22 different homes. He later joined
the U.S. Marine Corps, then briefly defected
to the U.S.S.R. before returning to the U.S.
At left, he poses in his backyard holding two
pro-Soviet newspapers in one hand and a
6.5-mm Carcano rifle in the other. His Russian wife Marina took the photo a few weeks
before Oswald apparently tried and failed to
gun down U.S. Army General Edwin Walker.
In November of that year, he succeeded in
assassinating President John F. Kennedy.

Charles Manson Is Arraigned
In a California Court

AP PHOTOGRAPHER
Los Angeles • Dec. 11, 1969

In its early years, the hippie movement
seemed winningly innocent, even child-
like, but by the end of the '60s a darker side
emerged, as more and more young people
who shunned "straight" society cast their
lot with unsavory characters like Manson.
The charismatic jailbird turned cult guru
surrounded himself with adoring lackeys,
mostly female, who were so deeply misguided
as to commit two sets of multiple murders at
his command. Above, Manson is arraigned
on charges of conspiring to commit murder.

Andy Warhol and Edie Sedgwick

STEVE SCHAPIRO
New York City • circa 1965

Some artists need a muse to inspire them, and the extent of Warhol's devotion to his hip young society friend is manifest in this photo. Warhol's investigation of the interplay between media and celebrity ("In the future everyone will be world famous for 15 minutes") seems increasingly prescient in an age when YouTube, Facebook and reality TV create instant overnight superstars. Warhol died in 1987, far too early to design the cover when TIME caught up with his vision in 2006 and named "You" as the Person of the Year.

Truman Capote's Black And White Ball

ELLIOTT ERWITT
New York City • Nov. 28, 1966

Without question, Capote's masked ball at the Plaza Hotel was *the* high-society event of the '60s. The writer was riding the acclaim he earned for his 1965 novel-length exercise in journalism, *In Cold Blood,* which helped establish the true-crime genre as a literary form, when he invited 500 of the era's glitterati to his lavish event. Among those attending were a pair whose recent marriage puzzled just about everyone, perhaps including themselves: Mia Farrow, 21, and Frank Sinatra, 50, divorced two years after they wed.

Fidel Castro and Nikita Khrushchev

MARTY LEDERHANDLER

United Nations, New York City • Sept. 20, 1960

When Castro's guerrilla warriors overthrew the corrupt government of Cuba's Fulgencio Batista on Jan. 1, 1959, few mourned the strongman's demise. At first, Castro presented himself as a simple fighter for his people's freedom. But by the end of 1960, Castro's sympathies were clear: he had embraced communism—and its worldwide leader, Soviet Premier Khrushchev.

Che Guevara at Workers' Awards Ceremony

RENE BURRI
Havana • 1963

Exuding charisma, a young Guevara, below, handed out awards to workers at a dinner honoring laborers in 1963. Even more than Castro, the Argentine physician would become the face of socialist revolution in the '60s. Unhappy as an administrator, Guevara left Cuba for Bolivia to join guerrillas in the jungle, where he was shot and killed by federal soldiers in 1967.

Lenny Bruce Is Arrested For Obscenity

UNKNOWN PHOTOGRAPHER
San Francisco • Oct. 4, 1961

He was born Leonard Alfred Schneider in Mineola, N.Y., a Long Island suburb of New York City. But the world got to know the stand-up comic by his stage name, Lenny Bruce. A defiant rebel from his first days of performing in the '50s, Bruce was a relentless critic of mainstream society with a master's degree in disdain; the nightclub stage was the pulpit from which he denounced society's hypocrisies. He wielded vulgarity as a sword against the Puritans and paid the price. After all, he declared, "life is a four-letter word."

Woody Allen Performs In a Nightclub

BILL RAY
Las Vegas • Dec. 5, 1966

If Bruce was comedy's Mr. Outside, obsessed with the world around him, Allen Stewart Konigsberg, a.k.a. Woody Allen, was Mr. Inside, harvesting laughs from his own tics, foibles and fears. The comedy genius from Brooklyn began his career writing short gags for other comics, then graduated to writing for Sid Caesar's popular 1950s TV show. By the '60s, he was introducing Americans to a type unknown to many: the brilliant, neurotic, nebbishy Jew who was only at home in city streets. "I am two with nature," he explained.

**Peter Fonda and Dennis
Hopper at Ease in Cannes**

MIRKINE
Cannes, France • May 1969

Hollywood's conservative producers were
stymied by the cultural changes of the 1960s:
early attempts to capture the emerging youth
culture on film, like *The Trip* (1967), were
laughable. Mike Nichols' *The Graduate* (1967)
finally caught the feel of the period, but it
wasn't until members of the new generation
were handed control of the process that the
counterculture hit the big screen. Fonda, the
writer, producer and star of 1969's hit *Easy
Rider,* a motorcycle saga, enjoyed the Cannes
Film Festival with director and co-star Hopper.

**John Wayne at Ease
Filming *The Undefeated***

JOHN DOMINIS
Hollywood or Durango, Mexico • 1969

No Hollywood star represented mainstream
American values in the '60s as stoutly as the
veteran western legend Wayne. The conservative cowboy star went behind the camera to
direct the defiantly patriotic *The Green Berets*
in 1968. The film was scorned by critics, but
Wayne scored a wonderful late-career success
in 1969 with his self-mocking star turn as
U.S. Marshal Rooster Cogburn in *True Grit,*
which put him on the cover of TIME and won
him his first Academy Award for Best Actor.
Above, Wayne takes a breather on location.

Events *of the 1960s*

Viewers Watch First Live Televised Presidential Debate

CORNELL CAPA
Chicago • Sept. 26, 1960

Television first began to take control of the living rooms and leisure hours of Americans in the early 1950s. By 1960, the riveting new medium was starting to transform politics as well. At left, a mesmerized crowd watches a historic moment in U.S. political history, as candidates Richard M. Nixon and John F. Kennedy square off in the first nationally televised presidential debate. Polls showed that Americans who listened to the debate on radio thought Nixon won, while those who watched on TV awarded the laurels to the more telegenic Kennedy.

Freedom Riders Prepare to Integrate a Bus Station

PAUL SCHUTZER
Outside Jackson • Miss., May 1, 1961

Energized by the Federal Government's growing support for their cause, black civil rights leaders began actively assaulting the bastions of racial segregation in the South in the early 1960s. "Freedom Riders" led the charge, risking beatings to integrate bus stations and lunch counters in segregated cities. Above, National Guard troops prepare to protect a group of Freedom Riders as they approach a segregated bus station.

Protesters Sit In at a Segregated Lunch Counter

FRED BLACKWELL
Jackson, Miss. • May 28, 1963

Learning from the publicity-savvy tactics of Mohandas Gandhi's successful crusade for India's independence decades before, civil rights protesters sought to create moments of high drama that would expose the inhumanity of racial repression in gripping images. This photo of whites vying to humiliate protesters at a segregated lunch counter neatly achieved its goal: it was the bigots who ultimately were shamed.

Police Train Fire Hoses on Protesters

CHARLES MOORE
Birmingham, Ala. • *May 1, 1963*

In 1963, civil rights leaders targeted Birmingham, Ala., one of the South's most segregated cities, as the focus of a major protest campaign aimed at integrating all city facilities. The nation was riveted by the demonstrations that followed, as the city's police turned water hoses and dogs on largely peaceful demonstrators. Above, marchers are barraged by high-velocity fire hoses. Martin Luther King Jr. was arrested while demonstrating on Good Friday, April 12; a letter he wrote to local ministers, now known as the "Letter from a Birmingham Jail," brilliantly laid out the case for integration.

Police Dogs Attack Civil Rights Marchers

CHARLES MOORE
Birmingham, Ala. • May 3, 1963

Police used German shepherds to attack demonstrators marching peacefully through downtown Birmingham in defiance of an ordinance passed by city authorities that declared the marches illegal. The scenes from Alabama shocked the nation, as protest leaders had hoped they would, and led the Kennedy White House to begin offering stronger federal support to the campaign for civil rights. Jacqueline Kennedy called Rev. King's wife Coretta Scott King on the telephone to express her concern during the civil rights leader's 11-day incarceration in a Birmingham jail.

41

The March on Washington Fills the National Mall

ROBERT W. KELLEY
Washington • Aug. 28, 1963

Taking advantage of the wave of sympathy for their cause that swept the nation following the dramatic events that took place in Birmingham in the spring of 1963, Rev. Martin Luther King Jr. and other civil rights leaders decided to showcase the extent of the support for their crusade with a massive March on Washington. The goal was to apply pressure on national leaders to pass civil rights legislation long bottled up in Congress.

The March on Washington was a success by anyone's measure: a massive throng estimated at 300,000 people filled the National Mall in a peaceful demonstration that was highlighted by King's stirring "I Have a Dream" address, in which he called for the "uncanceled check" of civil rights for African Americans to be passed at last. Noting the many white faces in the crowd, King said, "They have come to realize that their freedom is inextricably bound to our freedom. We cannot walk alone."

ROBERT W. KELLEY—TIME LIFE PICTURES

Local Authorities Appear in Court in Murder Case

BILL REED
Meridian, Miss. • Dec. 1, 1964

In June 1964 three civil rights volunteers were murdered outside Philadelphia, Miss. Neshoba County Sheriff Lawrence Rainey, on right, and 17 other men were arrested. Local citizens appeared to take the charges lightly, above, but ultimately seven of the accused were found guilty of civil rights violations, though none of murder. In 2005, thanks to crusading local journalist Jerry Mitchell, Edgar Ray Killen was found guilty of three charges of manslaughter in the case.

Martin Luther King Jr. Leads Voting March

UNKNOWN PHOTOGRAPHER
Montgomery, Ala. • March 1965

King became the most noted civil rights leader in the nation after he led the successful campaign to integrate the Montgomery, Ala., bus system in 1955-56, when he was only 27. In 1965 the Southern Christian Leadership Conference mounted a major effort to win voting rights for blacks in the South. At right, King and wife Coretta lead a group of marchers from Selma to the state capital in Montgomery to promote their cause, their voices raised in song.

Voters' March from Selma to Montgomery

JAMES KARALES
Montgomery, Ala. • March, 1965

This was the third of three marches that took place as black leaders highlighted the continuing denial of basic voting rights to African Americans in the South. The first protest took place on March 7, and participants leaving Selma were met by Alabama lawmen who used tear gas, clubs and whips to disperse the crowd. A second protest on March 9 was halted by Rev. Martin Luther King Jr. to avert similar conflicts. The third march, with the eyes of the nation watching, ended peacefully.

The image was brilliantly composed by Karales, who stood below the road in order to outline the marchers against a glowering sky. The three pace-setting figures in the lead, the American flag at center, the receding marchers in the distance: all create a powerful sense of intensity and forward momentum. "Like an idea whose time has come, not even the marching of mighty armies can halt us," declared protest leader King. President Lyndon B. Johnson signed the Voting Rights Act of 1965 into law five months after this march, on Aug. 6.

Summoning a Medical Evacuation Helicopter

ART GREENSPON

Hué, South Vietnam • April 1968

For Americans, the war in Vietnam was the defining international event of the 1960s, the wedge that divided the home front into old and young, hawks and doves, "patriots" and "traitors." As the nation fed more and more soldiers into Vietnam's killing fields and jungles, the long conflict was captured in a host of memorable images. Among them is this photo of a paratrooper of the 101st Airborne Division, lifting his arms as he summons a medical evacuation helicopter in the weeks after the Tet Offensive of early 1968. But his agonized pose is all too suggestive of America's plight in Southeast Asia: far from home, on the run and in search of aid from above that never seemed to arrive.

ART GREENSPON—AP IMAGES

A Buddhist Monk Self-Immolates

MALCOLM BROWNE
Saigon • June 11, 1963

Journalist Browne, one of the first U.S. correspondents to cover Vietnam, was a reporter rather than a photographer, but his photo of Buddhist monk Thích Quang Duc's self-immolation won a Pulitzer Prize in 1964. The dramatic suicide-by-fire, or *bonzo,* is tolerated in Mahayana Buddhism; it was followed by others, as Buddhist monks protested the crackdown on their religion by the regime led by Ngo Dinh Diem. Within five months of this event, the Diem regime had been toppled in a U.S.-supported coup. Journalist David Halberstam, an eyewitness, reported that the monk maintained his lotus position: "As he burned he never moved a muscle, never uttered a sound, his outward composure in sharp contrast to the wailing people around him."

South Vietnamese General Executes Prisoner

EDDIE ADAMS
Saigon • Feb. 1, 1968

Revenge was not served cold in Vietnam: above, General Nguyen Ngoc Loan, chief of the national police, fires his pistol into the head of suspected Viet Cong officer Nguyen Van Lem, soon after he was seized during the Tet Offensive. The dramatic photo of an execution sans trial won a Pulitzer Prize, helped undermine support among Americans for U.S. ally South Vietnam and disgraced Loan. Yet the photo haunted Adams, who sympathized with Loan and later wrote in TIME, "The general killed the Viet Cong; I killed the general with my camera. Still photographs are the most powerful weapon in the world. People believe them, but photographs do lie, even without manipulation. They are only half-truths." General Loan immigrated to the U.S.; he died in 1998.

Reaching Out

LARRY BURROWS
Nui Cay Tri, South Vietnam • Oct. 5, 1966

The foremost photojournalist of the Vietnam war was Briton Burrows; the picture at left is one of the most striking images from the conflict. Wounded and bandaged Marine Gunnery Sergeant Jeremiah Purdie, at left, is being led to join the stricken comrade on right, whose pose resembles a crucifixion, while they await medical evacuation. It was Purdie's third wound; after being treated on a hospital ship, he was sent back to the U.S.

Note the soldiers in the background; hardened by combat, they carry on with the minutiae of everyday life, ignoring the dramatic scene playing out in the foreground. After nine years of covering the conflict, Burrows died in 1971, along with three other photojournalists, when their helicopter was shot down over Laos. In 2008 their remains, found in 1996, were interred at the Newseum in Washington.

President Johnson Reacts to Tape from Vietnam

JACK KIGHTLINGER
Washington • July 31, 1968

Lyndon B. Johnson was one of the strongest of Presidents—in his domestic achievements. But in massively escalating the war in Vietnam, he misjudged his adversary, Ho Chi Minh. As U.S. casualties mounted, with no escape in sight, Johnson neared despair. At left, he reacts to a tape sent from Vietnam by his son-in-law, Captain Charles Robb, who spoke of his pain at losing brave young Americans under his command.

Bodies Lie in Ditch After My Lai Massacre

RONALD HAEBERLE
My Lai, Vietnam • March 16, 1968

This photograph, taken by an official Army photographer with his personal camera, offered damning evidence of the massacre committed by U.S. soldiers in My Lai in 1968 when it was first published in November 1969. For 18 months, the Army had hushed up the event, in which some 400 South Vietnamese civilians, primarily women and children, were brutally murdered by American troops.

**Assassination of President
John F. Kennedy**

ABRAHAM ZAPRUDER

Dallas • Nov. 22, 1963

The 20th century was the great age of cinema, but perhaps the most significant footage of the century was shot with a home-movie camera by amateur Zapruder, a garment executive who trained his lens on President Kennedy's motorcade as it passed through Dealey Plaza in Dallas during a goodwill trip to Texas. The frame above, No. 237 on the 26-sec. strip of film, shows Kennedy, struck from behind by

a bullet, involuntarily raising his arms, while wife Jackie turns toward him. At right, Mrs. Kennedy, perhaps seeking help or believing herself a target, scrambles onto the back of the limousine. Rights to the film were purchased by LIFE magazine correspondent Dick Stolley, and individual frames were published in its Nov. 29 issue. The original film is now in the collection of the U.S. National Archives.

Lyndon B. Johnson Takes the Oath of Office

CECIL STOUGHTON

Dallas • Nov. 22, 1963

In the chaotic hours after the assassination of President Kennedy, Vice President Johnson, also in the motorcade, was taken to the hospital along with Kennedy, then was whisked to the safety of Air Force One, parked at Dallas' Love Field. Federal judge Sarah T. Hughes administered the oath as 27 people crowded into the cabin. Stoughton, the only photojournalist present, recorded the most dramatic swearing-in ever taken by a U.S. President. Jacqueline Kennedy insisted on being present, though her late husband's blood was still evident on her pink Chanel suit.

Jack Ruby Shoots Lee Harvey Oswald

BOB JACKSON
Dallas • Nov. 24, 1963

Compounding the agony of a nation after the assassination of President
Kennedy, the chief suspect in the case, Oswald, was shot by Ruby, a local
nightclub operator, two days after the President's murder. Dallas *Times
Herald* photographer Jackson, 29, won a Pulitzer Prize for this photo. Two
days before, Jackson had been traveling in the presidential motorcade and
heard shots ring out from an upper-floor window in the Texas School Book
Depository Building. Turning his head, he saw a rifle barrel in a sixth-floor
window, but when he went to snap a photo, his camera was out of film.

John Kennedy Jr. Salutes His Father's Casket

STAN STEARNS
Washington • Nov. 25, 1963

John F. Kennedy's funeral was held on Monday, Nov. 25. Above, the President's family stands on the steps of St. Matthew's Cathedral in Washington after the service. The President's son John Jr. had been taught by his father to salute the American flag when he saw it. Prompted by his mother, he did so when his father's horse-drawn, flag-draped casket passed by, a moment that moved the nation. It was the youngster's third birthday.

Jacqueline Kennedy Receives the U.S. Flag

UPI PHOTOGRAPHER
Washington • Nov. 25, 1963

At right, Mrs. Kennedy holds the flag that covered her husband's casket as Robert Kennedy and Richard Cardinal Cushing of Boston stand by; her grace under pressure helped steady a nation in shock. As TIME later noted, "She also refused to take tranquilizers, fearing they would blunt her reactions and interfere with her planning— because plan the funeral she did. The riderless horse, the eternal flame, the wailing Irish bagpipe—all were her idea."

Martin Luther King Jr. Is Assassinated in Memphis

JOSEPH LOUW
Memphis, Tenn. • April 4, 1968

Civil rights leader Andrew Young and other witnesses point in the direction of rifle fire in the moments after King was shot by James Earl Ray as the civil rights leader stood on the balcony of the Lorraine Motel in Memphis.

The night before, King had delivered an eerily prescient speech to the city's striking sanitation workers, whose cause had brought him to Memphis. "I just want to do God's will. And He's allowed me to go up to the mountain. And I've looked over. And I've seen the Promised Land. I may not get there with you. But I want you to know tonight, that we, as a people, will get to the Promised Land."

JOSEPH LOUW—TIME LIFE PICTURES

Robert F. Kennedy
Campaigns in Philadelphia

CONSTANTINE MANOS
Philadelphia • April 2, 1968

U.S. Senator Kennedy entered the 1968 presidential race only weeks before President Lyndon Johnson announced he would not seek the Democratic nomination—and thus angering antiwar activists who had been supporting the lonely crusade of Senator Eugene McCarthy. But Kennedy's charisma and status as the brother and closest confidant of the late President electrified the nation's voters. Above, he campaigns in downtown Philadelphia.

Senator Kennedy Is
Assassinated in Los Angeles

BILL EPPRIDGE
Los Angeles • June 5, 1968

When Kennedy won the critical California primary on June 5, he became the front runner for the Democratic presidential nomination. But shortly after delivering a victory address at the Ambassador Hotel, the Senator was shot to death by Sirhan Sirhan, a Palestinian immigrant. At right, busboy Juan Romero comforts Kennedy, who inquired of him: "Is everybody O.K.?" Romero replied in the affirmative before Kennedy lost consciousness.

Fires Set Amid Rioting Devastate Detroit

DECLAN HAUN
Detroit • July 1967

The early 1960s saw real progress for U.S. African Americans, as civil rights activists fought for—and won—legislation removing many of the shameful injustices of the past. But beginning in 1965, when the heavily black Watts neighborhood of Los Angeles exploded in rioting, many of the nation's cities saw marginalized blacks rising up to torch their own neighborhoods. No city was harder hit than Detroit, whose summer 1967 riots left 41 people dead, 2,700 businesses sacked, vast swaths of the city burned to the ground— and sent whites streaming out of the city and into the suburbs, further exacerbating the city's racial and economic divisions.

A National Guard Soldier Patrols Newark

MEL FINKELSTEIN
Newark, N.J. • July 14, 1967

Newark also went up in flames in the summer of '67.
As TIME reported from Detroit, the urban riots not
only divided blacks and whites; they also created deep
rifts within the black community itself. "The mobs
cared nothing for 'Negro leadership' ... looters screamed
at a well-dressed Negro psychiatrist: 'We're going to get
you rich niggers next!' " The magazine's view: "They
[blacks] have despaired finally—some this summer,
others much earlier—of hope in white America."

Students Take Over Columbia University

DENNIS CARUSO
New York City • April 25, 1968

In the bellwether year 1968, long-standing divisions on college campuses flared up across the nation. New York City's Columbia University faced the most intense crisis, as students protesting the university's building of a student gym on playgrounds used by local blacks stormed the office of president Grayson Kirk, took over five university buildings, held three college officials hostage for 24 hours and forced the suspension of all classes. Above, student leader Mark Rudd is interviewed in front of President Kirk's occupied office.

Students Battle at Columbia

UNKNOWN PHOTOGRAPHER
New York City • April 27, 1968

The battle at Columbia involved the entire community; 30 professors barred police from ejecting students who had taken over Low Library. Outside, students opposing the protests, including athletes, formed a cordon to starve out the occupiers. When demonstrators tried to break through them, a melee ensued, above. Eventually, New York City police were called in to take control of the campus.

LIN SINTAY—UPI—BETTMANN CORBIS

Chicago Police Use Brute Force Against Protesters

LIN SINTAY
Chicago • Aug. 28, 1968

If ever there was a year from hell in the U.S., 1968 was it. Americans were riven by the Vietnam War and by race, age and cultural values. On March 31, a beleaguered President Lyndon Johnson announced he would not run for re-election; within nine weeks, two young forces for change, the Rev. Martin Luther King Jr. and Senator Robert F. Kennedy, had been shot dead. The anguish continued at the Democratic National Convention in Chicago, where police beat young protesters in the street, while others chanted: "The whole world is watching." To America's shame, that was true.

A Demonstrator Defies the Police

PERRY C. RIDDLE
Chicago • Aug. 28, 1968

A young man extends a greeting to Chicago authorities: a subsequent commission called the convention events "a police riot," while noting that the cops had been provoked. TIME totaled up the score a week later: "They [the protesters] left Chicago more as victors than as victims ... their strategy became one of calculated provocation. The aim was to irritate the police and the party bosses so intensely that their reactions would look like those of mindless brutes and skull-busters. After all the blood, sweat and tear gas, the dissidents had pretty well succeeded in doing just that."

PERRY C. RIDDLE—CHICAGO DAILY NEWS

JAMES MCDIVITT—NASA

Astronaut Alan Shepard Approaches Launchpad

RALPH MORSE
Cape Canaveral, Fla. • May 5, 1961

Shepard, one of the original seven astronauts in NASA's Mercury program, was chosen to be America's first man in space, riding a capsule dubbed *Freedom 7*, sent aloft by a Redstone rocket. Here he strides to the launch gantry to board the craft. His suborbital flight lasted just over 15 minutes—and seemed a feeble response to the rival Soviets, who had sent Yuri Gagarin on a complete orbit around the planet three weeks earlier.

Edward White Takes the First U.S. Spacewalk

JAMES McDIVITT
Earth orbit • June 3, 1965

NASA's Mercury program was followed by a much more substantial effort, the Gemini program, which sent two men into space on each mission for days at a time. During the Gemini 4 mission, pilot White became the first American to walk in space, hovering weightless and tethered to the craft by a lifeline for 23 minutes. Mission Commander McDivitt snapped this photo from within the Gemini capsule.

Earthrise from The Moon

WILLIAM ANDERS
Lunar orbit • Dec. 24, 1968

This photo became one of the iconic images of the late '60s. Showing Earth from a perspective never seen before, it helped add urgency to the new environmental awareness that emerged at the end of the decade. It was taken on the Apollo 8 mission at the end of 1968, a run-up to the moon landing. As three Americans orbited the moon, they read from the Book of Genesis on Christmas Eve, as Earthlings listened—a final requiem for a turbulent year.

The U.S. Flag Flies On the Moon

NEIL ARMSTRONG
Lunar surface • July 20, 1969

In 1961 President John F. Kennedy challenged NASA to land men on the moon before 1970. The space agency beat the goal by five months when astronauts Armstrong and Edwin (Buzz) Aldrin clambered down the stairs of landing craft *Eagle* and onto the lunar surface. The world watched, enthralled, as the two bounded around the low-gravity satellite and planted the Stars and Stripes on the moon. A metal bar at top kept the banner upright.

Roman Catholic Cardinals At Vatican Council II

HANK WALKER
Vatican City • Oct. 11, 1962

When portly, personable Angelo Cardinal Roncalli was elected Pope at age 76 in 1958, many thought he would be a placeholder. But Pope John XXIII surprised his vast worldwide flock when he summoned Catholic Cardinals to Rome for a rare council intended to refresh and update the church. The Second Vatican Council overhauled the ancient religion in ways that remain highly controversial, though Pope John did not live to see those changes.

Billy Graham Undertakes A Mission to Africa

JAMES BURKE
Kisumu, Kenya • March 7, 1960

Graham first rose to fame in the early 1950s, and by the '60s he was easily America's best-known Protestant evangelist. The master of a Southern Baptist preaching tradition that emphasized ringing, old-fashioned oratory and a final "altar call" that invited converts to come forward and testify to their faith, Graham traveled the U.S. and the world bearing his message. Here he meets with members of Kenya's indigenous Luo people on a mission to Africa.

LEFT: HANK WALKER—TIME LIFE PICTURES. RIGHT: JAMES BURKE—TIME LIFE PICTURES

77

Muhammad Ali Knocks Out Sonny Liston

NEIL LEIFER
Lewiston, Maine • May 25, 1965

Gearing up to fight Sonny Liston, 33, for the heavyweight title of the world in 1964, Cassius Clay, then only 22, concocted a memorable brag, incorporating a phrase used by his cornerman Bundini Brown: "Float like a butterfly, sting like a bee/ Your hands can't hit what your eyes can't see." The "Louisville Lip" made good on his boast, taking Liston's title away in six rounds. The rematch in 1965 left fans feeling stung: Liston went down in the first round, at right, and was counted out, though Clay, who had now changed his name to Muhammad Ali, never seemed to hit him hard. Fans accused Liston of throwing the fight by succumbing to a "phantom punch" that just about no one saw.

NEIL LEIFER

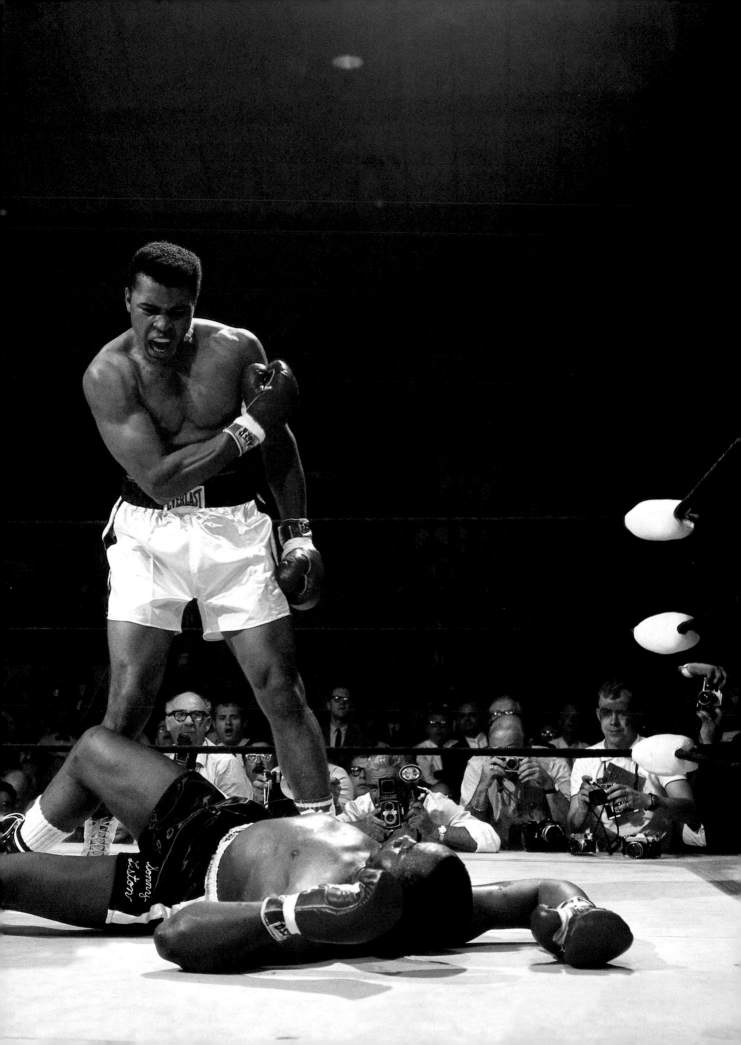

WALTER IOOSS JR.—SPORTS ILLUSTRATED—GETTY IMAGES

GEORGE LONG—SPORTS ILLUSTRATED—GETTY IMAGES

The "Amazin' Mets" Win the World Series

WALTER IOOSS JR.
New York City • Oct. 16, 1969

The New York Mets had served as comic relief for the National League since they were created as an expansion team in 1961. TIME called them "incontestably the most ludicrous team in the chronicle of baseball." But in 1969 the young squad, led by pitchers Tom Seaver, 24, and Nolan Ryan, 22, beat the slugging Baltimore Orioles in the Series. Above, catcher Jerry Grote and pitcher Jerry Koosman taste the glory.

Bill Russell and Wilt Chamberlain

GEORGE LONG
Inglewood, Calif. • April 23, 1969

Recipe for a classic NBA final: the Boston Celtics vs. the Los Angeles Lakers. And when the two centers were legends—Russell in green and "Wilt the Stilt" in yellow and blue—well, it's enough to make you forget about the short shorts worn back in the day, which the players called "Marilyn Monroes." Wilt got off this shot against Russell, but the Celtics beat Wilt, Jerry West, Elgin Baylor and the Lakers in seven games.

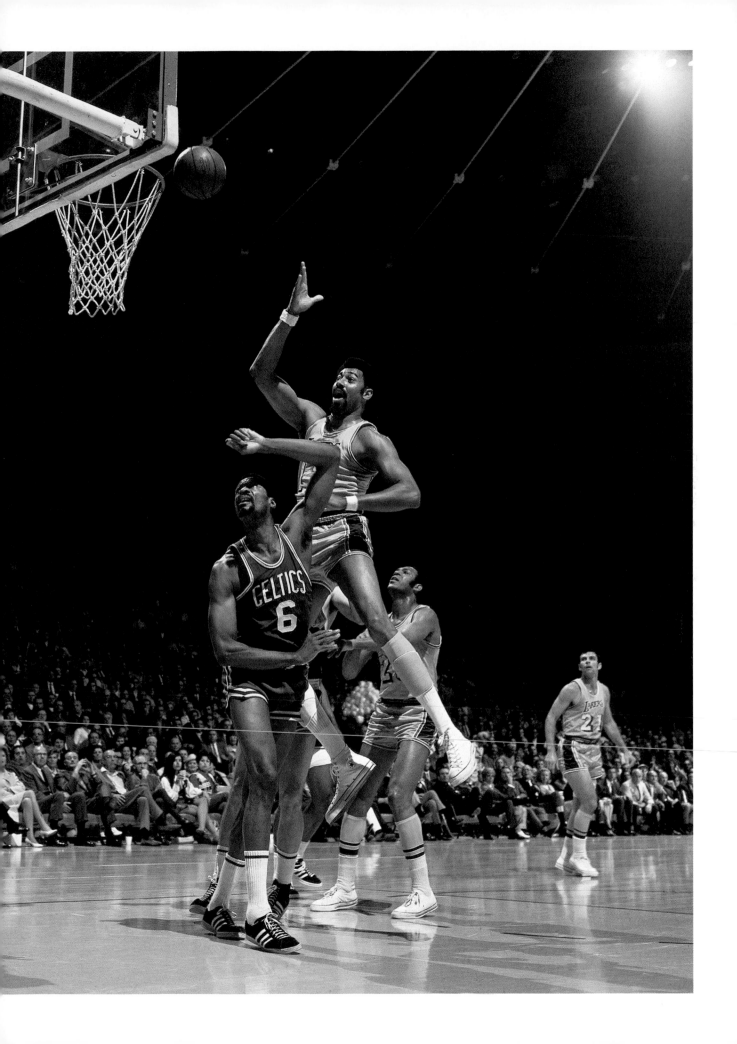

**Joe Cocker's Band Prepares to Play
At the Woodstock Music & Art Fair**

ELLIOTT LANDY
Bethel, N.Y. • Aug. 17, 1969

"Don't trust anyone over 30," was one of the rallying cries of kids in the '60s—and TIME
magazine was a venerable 46 years old when the hippie movement reached escape
velocity at the Woodstock festival, held over three days in a 600-acre pasture in upstate
New York. But TIME's original report of the decade's biggest party got it right: "The
festival turned out to be history's largest happening. As the moment when the special

culture of U.S. youth of the '60s openly displayed its strength, appeal and power, it may well rank as one of the significant political and sociological events of the age." That it did. Turning soggy fields into mudslides and shrugging off inadequate infrastructure and bad acid, some 400,000 attendees enjoyed the music of Jimi Hendrix, the Who and more. As Joni Mitchell later wrote, "Everywhere there was song and celebration."

East German Soldier Defects to the West

PETER LEIBING
Berlin • Aug. 15, 1961

Cold war tensions peaked in the early 1960s, when the U.S. and the U.S.S.R. clashed in two hot spots, divided Berlin and Fidel Castro's Cuba. Above, East German border guard Conrad Schumann, 19, hops over a fence dividing East and West Berlin, even as a wall dividing the two halves of the occupied city was being built at the order of Soviet Premier Nikita Khrushchev.

Aerial Photos Show Missile Bases in Cuba
PHOTO FROM U-2 RECONNAISSANCE PLANE
Cuba • Oct. 23, 1962

In October 1962, photos taken by an American U-2 spy plane
showed bases for Soviet missiles under construction in Cuba,
only 90 miles from Florida—a retaliation by the U.S.S.R.
for U.S. missiles based in Turkey and Italy that could reach
Moscow. The photos, shown in TIME and other publications,
sparked a chilling diplomatic crisis, which was resolved when
Russia agreed to withdraw its missiles from Cuba and the U.S.
did the same in Europe. The images also served notice that
new technology was revolutionizing the art of reconnaissance.

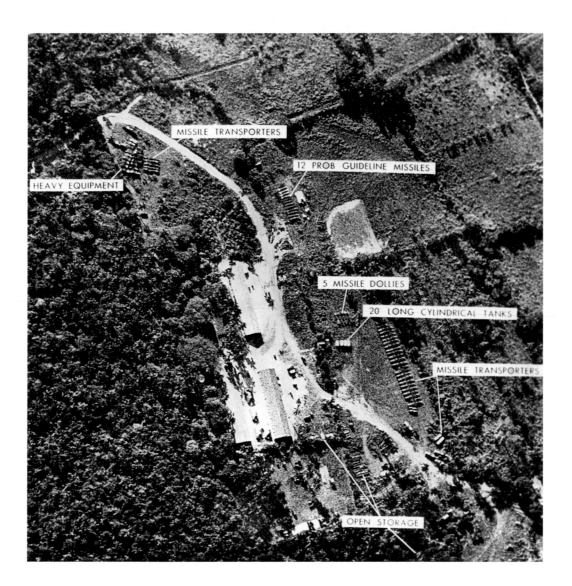

Czech Rebels
Seize a Soviet Tank

JOSEF KOUDELKA
Prague • August 1968

Squirming since the end of
World War II within the tight
grip of Soviet rule, Czechs and
Slovaks entertained buoyant
dreams of freedom during the
period known as the Prague
Spring early in 1968. Czecho-
slovakia's leader, Alexander
Dubcek, encouraged a welcome
thaw in those months, and
citizens greeted the restoration
of free speech with an explosion
of creative expression.

By late summer, Soviet
leader Leonid Brezhnev had
seen enough: on Aug. 20 he sent
200,000 Warsaw Pact troops
and some 2,000 tanks rolling
into the nation to arrest Dubcek
and restore Soviet authority. At
left, rebels waving the national
flag have put one tank out of
commission, but by wintertime,
the clampdown was complete.

Egyptian Prisoners in the Six-Day War
UNKNOWN PHOTOGRAPHER
Sinai Peninsula, Egypt • June 8, 1967

Captured Egyptian soldiers on their way to a detention camp, right, pass
Israeli troops heading for the front lines during the Six-Day War. The
conflict erupted after a long period of escalating tensions in the region. When
Egypt, Jordan and Syria began major troop buildups on their borders, Israel
launched a pre-emptive strike on June 5. After early air raids wiped out the
Arabs' Soviet-supplied air forces, Israel's ground army won a series of battles.
At the end of the brief war, Israel took charge of a host of occupied territories,
including the Sinai Peninsula, Gaza Strip, the West Bank, East Jerusalem and
the Golan Heights. Their fate would shape the region's politics for decades.

Yasser Arafat Emerges

GENEVIEVE CHAUVEL
Jordan • April 1969

TIME readers encountered an unfamiliar face on the cover of the magazine's Dec. 13, 1968, issue. Introducing this new figure on the world scene, TIME said, "Arabs have come to idolize Mohammed ("Yasser") Arafat, a leader of El Fatah fedayeen who has emerged as the most visible spokesman for the commandos. An intense, secretive and determined Palestinian, he is enthusiastically portrayed by the admiring Arab press as a latter-day Saladin, with the Israelis supplanting the Crusaders as the hated-and-feared-foe." Arafat told TIME, "Please, no personality cult. I am only a soldier. Our leader is Palestine. Our road is the road of death and sacrifice to win back our homeland."

Blacks Flee Gunfire From White Police

IAN BERRY
Sharpeville, South Africa
March 21, 1960

Throughout the 1960s, South Africa's minority white population maintained a firm grip on the nation's black majority through the policy of apartheid, which kept races strictly segregated. In March 1960, black leaders called for a nationwide protest against the use of passbooks, ID papers that had to be shown by blacks upon leaving or entering the bogus bantustans, or "homelands," into which they were restricted. In Sharpeville, some 28 miles southwest of Johannesburg, a peaceful demonstration got out of hand, and white police began firing wildly into the crowds of unarmed black protesters.

At left, blacks flee the gunfire; white police can be seen in the background, shooting from the tops of armored cars. By day's end, 69 blacks were dead and more than 200 were wounded. Nations around the world denounced the regime's harsh rule, and antiapartheid leader Nelson Mandela publicly burned his passbook in protest.

French Students Battle Police in the Streets

BRUNO BARBEY
Paris • May 6, 1968

Rebellion against the established order wasn't confined to the U.S. in the late 1960s, as the cultural divisions of the period sparked upheavals around the globe. In France, college students rose up against academic authorities, and labor unions soon joined them in a larger revolt against the authoritarian regime of Charles de Gaulle. The World War II hero survived rioting in the streets in 1968 but resigned in 1969.

Northern Irish Police Monitor a Protest March

UNKNOWN PHOTOGRAPHER
Londonderry, Northern Ireland • Aug. 13, 1969

In Northern Ireland, the six counties of Ulster province that remained part of the U.K. after Ireland's 1921 partition, religious differences sparked battles in the streets between minority Catholics and majority Protestants loyal to the Queen. At right, police have set up barricades to stop a Catholic protest march. But the nation's bitter cycle of hatred and violence would not be halted until the very end of the century.

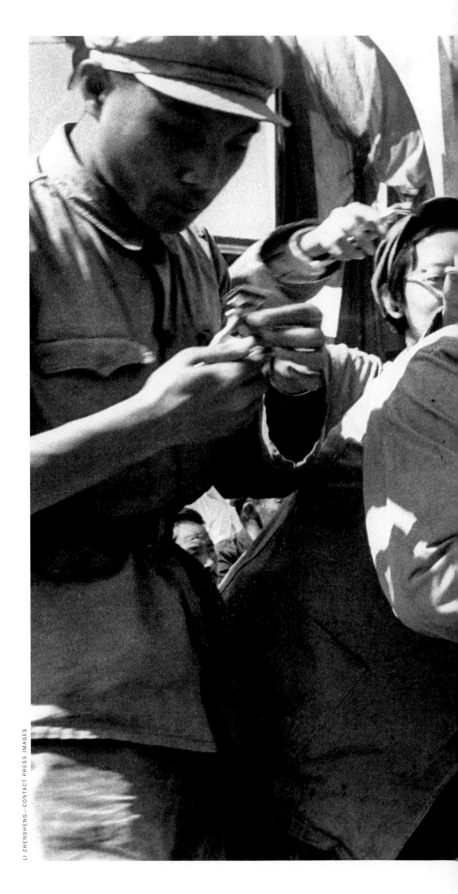

LI ZHENSHENG—CONTACT PRESS IMAGES

Red Guards Humiliate a Provincial Governor

LI ZHENSHENG
Heilongjiang, China • 1967

Mao Zedong's China had barely recovered from the disastrous years of the Great Leap Forward—the late-'50s economic strategy that turned out to be Two Great Steps Back—before Chairman Mao launched another campaign that sent his nation into a decade of civil unrest verging on anarchy. "Bombard the headquarters!" Mao urged his devout followers as he sought to oust his conservative foes within the Communist Party hierarchy. The Red Guards, young men and women nurtured all their lives on a diet of propaganda that deified Mao and his *Little Red Book*, were only too happy to do so. Party leaders once held in high esteem were now set upon by Red Guards and publicly humiliated in "struggle sessions" or sent to be "re-educated" by performing manual labor in the countryside. China would not regain its bearings until after Mao's death in 1976. At right, Governor Li Fanwu of Heilongjiang Province is given a public haircut while wearing a sign branding him a "careerist."

Currents *of the 1960s*

Beatles Fans Storm Buckingham Palace

UNKNOWN PHOTOGRAPHER
London • Oct. 26, 1965

Pity the poor bobbies tasked with keeping screaming Beatles fans in check outside Buckingham Palace when the four musicians were awarded honors by Queen Elizabeth II for their contributions to British society. Beatlemania was still in full bloom at this moment, but the days of the Fab Four would soon come to an end, as the restless artists refused to continue playing their well-polished roles as lovable moptops and chose to follow the path of artistic and personal growth.

As a 1967 TIME cover story declared after the stunning success of the group's *Sgt. Pepper's Lonely Hearts Club Band* album, "Rich and secure enough to go on repeating themselves—or to do nothing at all—they have exercised a compulsion for growth, change and experimentation."

**Chubby Checker and
A Fan Do the Twist**

RALPH CRANE
Los Angeles • 1961

"Come on, baby, let's do the Twist," sang the appealing Checker in 1960, and Americans by the millions quickly consented and began to gyrate. The Twist was the first great dance craze of the '60s, but it was also one of the last of a dying breed: Checker's hit was a cleaned-up cover of the gutsier 1959 original by rhythm-and-blues artist Hank Ballard. When the Beatles and Bob Dylan began to write brilliant songs expressing their own views, they made such prefab, pre–Fab Four pop seem dated (well, except to Monkees fans).

**Rudolf Nureyev and
Margot Fonteyn**

UNKNOWN PHOTOGRAPHER
London • March 8, 1963

Nureyev's thrillingly high leaps— and thrillingly high Tatar cheekbones—had made him the foremost male dancer at Russia's famed Kirov Ballet. Then the charismatic star, 23, defected to the West while on tour in Paris in 1961, electrifying the world. Nureyev soon joined Britain's Royal Ballet company, where he quickly teamed up with the troupe's star ballerina, Fonteyn, then 42, to form one of the greatest pairs in ballet history. Above, they rehearse *Marguerite and Armand,* created specifically for them by Frederick Ashton.

99

LEFT: BRUCE DAVIDSON—MAGNUM PHOTOS. RIGHT: MICHAEL OCHS ARCHIVE—GETTY IMAGES

The Supremes Rehearsing At Motown Studios

BRUCE DAVIDSON
Detroit • 1965

Black artists had given American music its soul and tempo since the early 19th century, yet even such stars as Louis Armstrong and Duke Ellington fought racial discrimination. But Berry Gordy's Motown Studios in Detroit made black music tops with listeners of all stripes in the 1960s. Gordy's hit factory cultivated such brilliant songwriters and performers as Stevie Wonder, the Temptations and Smokey Robinson. And he made the Supremes—from left, Diana Ross, Florence Ballard and Mary Wilson—into superstars.

The Beach Boys Perform On ABC's *Shindig*

UNKNOWN PHOTOGRAPHER
Los Angeles • Dec. 17, 1964

No artists captured the exuberance of the early 1960s better than California's Beach Boys, a family band whose first hits celebrated hot rods, surfing and *California Girls*. The genius of the group was Brian Wilson, center; at right are singer Mike Love (the Wilsons' cousin) and drummer Dennis Wilson; at left are Carl Wilson and Al Jardine. Emotionally frail, Brian Wilson suffered a breakdown in 1964 and retired from touring, retreating to the studio to write more challenging songs like *Good Vibrations* and *Surf's Up*.

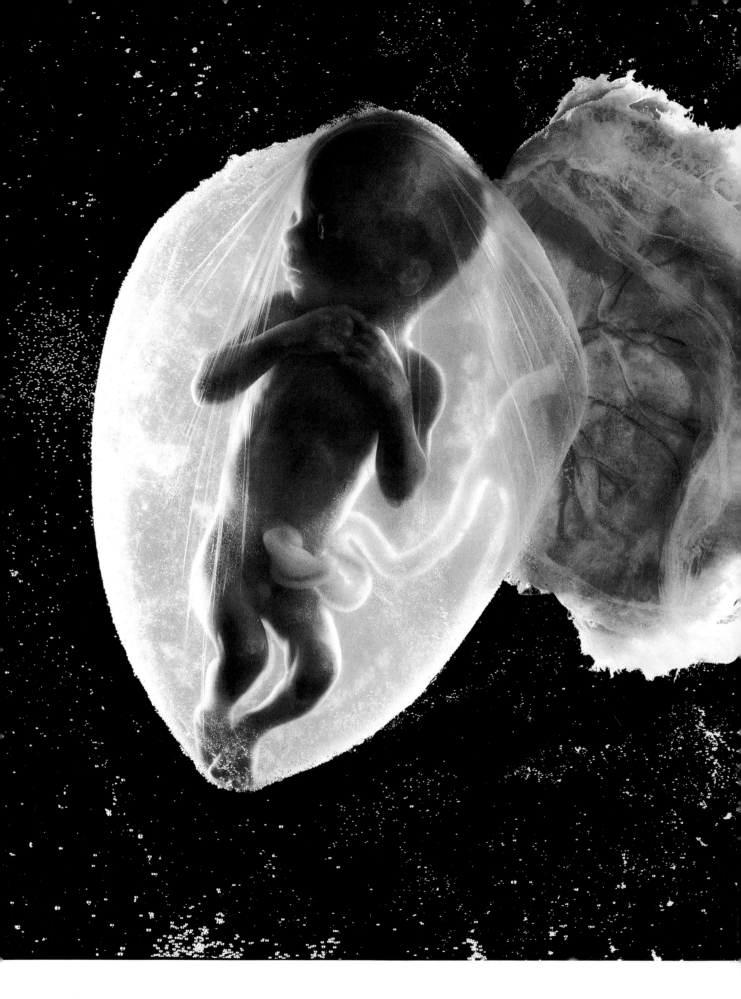

LENNART NILSSON—SCANPIX

18-Week-Old Human Embryo in the Womb

LENNART NILSSON
Published April 30, 1965

The 1960s saw great strides in the exploration of outer space, but one photographer dazzled the world with his revelations of inner space. Nilsson's pioneering images, using new medical technology such as endoscopes small enough to fit into human veins, showed viewers a world they had never seen, the growth and development of human embryos inside the womb from the instant of conception. When the Swedish photographer's first 16-page photo portfolio appeared in LIFE magazine in the spring of 1965, it startled the world and the images became a signature of the era; director Stanley Kubrick appropriated them in the famously enigmatic conclusion of his classic 1968 film, *2001: A Space Odyssey.* Later, the pictures would play a role in the debates over the ethics of abortion that followed the U.S. Supreme Court's 1973 ruling legalizing the practice in the U.S.

George Plimpton's Cocktail Party

CORNELL CAPA
New York City • Nov. 30, 1963

No, this isn't a backstage shot from *Mad Men;* it's a cocktail party at the Upper East Side apartment of *Paris Review* editor George Plimpton, who would carve out an amusing sideline for himself in the '60s as a sort of Everyman of sports, beginning with his popular 1966 book recounting his attempts to play football with the NFL's Detroit Lions, *Paper Lion.* The cattle call of the chattering classes shown above features a host of notables; we won't name them all, but for those who enjoy *Where's Waldo?,* here are some of the attendees: Ralph Ellison, Peter Matthiessen, Sidney Lumet, Arthur Kopit, Arthur Penn and Truman Capote. Host Plimpton is seated in the left foreground, next to literary agent Maggie Abbott.

Allen Ginsberg at the Human Be-In

LISA LAW

San Francisco • Jan. 14, 1967

Ginsberg's defining work *Howl* may have been published in 1956, but the poet was still flying high in the '60s. Above, he chants mantras and practices the politics of ecstasy at the first-ever Be-In at Golden Gate Park. The disciple of Walt Whitman and his "barbaric yawp" easily made the transition from beatnik to hippie.

"Goldwater Girls" Rally Before the Republican National Convention, 1964

JOHN DOMINIS
San Francisco • July 1964

In the accelerated atmosphere of the 1960s, four years could seem a lifetime. In the period between the 1964 and 1968 presidential elections, lovable boxer Cassius Clay became defiant Muslim Muhammad Ali, the Beatles exchanged "I want to hold your hand" for "I'd love to turn you on"—and a full-fledged counterculture took shape in the U.S., primarily fed by divisions over President Lyndon Johnson's rapid escalation of the Vietnam War. There were some 16,000 U.S. troops in the southeast Asian nation in 1964 and more than 550,000 by '68. Johnson's huge victory over conservative Republican Barry Goldwater in 1964 paved the way for his controversial domestic program, the Great Society.

Protesters Rally at the Democratic National Convention, 1968

ART SHAY
Chicago • August 1968

The term baby boomer had yet to be coined when TIME took note of the major generational shift that was transforming U.S. life by naming Americans "25 and Under" the Man of the Year for 1966. Said the magazine: "Never have the young been so assertive or so articulate, so well educated or so worldly. Predictably, they are a highly independent breed, and—to adult eyes—their independence has made them highly unpredictable. This is not just a new generation, but a new kind of generation."

Joan Baez Sings at Berkeley

TED STRESHINSKY
Berkeley, Calif. • Nov. 20, 1964

College campuses became hotbeds of dissent against mainstream society in the '60s. The trend became more pronounced as the Johnson Administration escalated the War in Vietnam in 1965, but the student-power movement first attracted national attention a year earlier at the University of California, Berkeley, when the Free Speech Movement served notice to college administrators that students would no longer be content to take a passive role in the politics of campus life. Folksinger Baez, like many young people, was radicalized by the war. In 1967 TIME called her "the nightingale of nonviolence."

Protesters March on the Pentagon

BERNIE BOSTON
Washington • Oct. 21, 1967

This photo of a young Vietnam war protester deploying "flower power" against National Guard soldiers memorably captures the era's divisions, often simplified as a struggle between old and young—except that in this case the buzz-cut soldiers and the long-haired students are members of the same generation. The occasion was the first nationwide protest against the War in Vietnam, which drew more than 100,000 people, including antiwar activists Benjamin Spock and Normal Mailer, to "March on the Pentagon." The resulting clashes between authorities and demonstrators were the first major instances of civil violence in the capital since the Bonus March riots of 1932.

Black Panthers at a Protest Rally

STEPHEN SHAMES
Oakland, Calif. • July 28, 1968

"I am America," declared Muhammad Ali in 1965, while under fire as
"un-American" for joining the Black Muslims. "I am the part you won't
recognize, but get used to me. Black, confident, cocky. My name, not yours.
My religion, not yours. My goals, my own. Get used to me." Many proud young
blacks who shared Ali's views joined the Black Panthers, a quasi-military Black
Power group founded in 1966 by Huey Newton and Bobby Seale. Above,
Panthers attend a rally demanding the release of "Minister of Defense" Newton,
then standing trial for killing a policeman. The charges were eventually dropped.

U.S. Athletes Stage Protest at Olympic Games

UNKNOWN PHOTOGRAPHER
Mexico City • Oct. 16, 1968

No year in the 1960s was more beset with turmoil and ill feelings than 1968. That year the ongoing racial divisions in U.S. society were highlighted on the global stage at the Mexico City Olympic Games when gold medalist Tommie Smith, center, and bronze medalist John Carlos capped their success in the 200-m race by displaying the Black Power salute on the awards platform. The show of protest was met with blistering scorn by many Americans, and the two sprinters faced death threats when they returned home. Australian silver medalist Peter Norman wore a badge showing his sympathy with their cause.

The Kiss

LARRY KEENAN
Los Altos Hills, Calif. • 1969

Like the "flapper" girls who put the roar in the Roaring Twenties, the hippies who appeared in the 1960s represented an entirely new element in American life. Scorning material possessions and devoted to rock music, "peace and love" (and pot), they managed to bewilder, amuse, annoy and frighten their elders all at once. Mission accomplished!

Hippie Commune

EVE ARNOLD
Drop City, N.M. • 1968

The hippie counterculture first emerged in San Francisco, New York City and Los Angeles, but in the late '60s a powerful back-to-the-earth movement took hold. Hippies shunned the nation's big cities to head for the hills, aided by such how-to guides as Stewart Brand's *Whole Earth Catalog* and heeding the prophet of simple living, writer Wendell Berry.

The Hog Farm Commune's Bus of Many Colors

LISA LAW
El Rito, N.M. • July 4, 1968

"You're either on the bus or off the bus," Merry Prankster guru Ken Kesey explained to Tom Wolfe in the writer's classic 1968 exploration of psychedelic tomfoolery, *The Electric Kool-Aid Acid Test.* Translation: You're either hip or square. The Pranksters may have been the first to buy an old school bus and turn it into a moveable feast of Day-Glo swirls, but they soon had company, including members of the Hog Farm commune, right, whose *Road Hog* joined a Fourth of July parade in New Mexico in 1968. The Beatles eventually got on board the trend with their Magical Mystery Tour of England in September 1967. The Pranksters' original bus, *Furthur,* broke down in 1967 and is currently rusting and rusticating on an Oregon farm.

Merry Pranksters at the "Acid Graduation"

TED STRESHINSKY
San Francisco • Oct. 31, 1966

Novelist Ken Kesey, with microphone, wrote
One Flew Over the Cuckoo's Nest (1962) about
his experiences working in a mental ward, at
times under the influence of the psychedelic
drug LSD (lysergic acid diethylamide). Kesey
first took "acid" as a guinea pig in medical
experiments, and he championed its use. When
LSD was outlawed in California in 1966, Kesey
and his Merry Pranksters staged a mock "acid
graduation" and took their scene underground.

Dancing at the Avalon Ballroom

TED STRESHINSKY
San Francisco • circa 1966-67

Fledgling hippies flocked to San Francisco in the
mid-'60s to join the psychedelic revolution; at
right, a dancer gets in the groove at the Avalon
Ballroom. The scene peaked with the "Summer
of Love" in 1967, when swarms of unemployed
street kids overwhelmed city social services. As
TIME reported, the city's original hippies were
so outraged by the newcomers that they held a
satirical "Death of Hip" funeral in October 1967,
bidding farewell to their waning high times.

Reverie
ROY LICHTENSTEIN
1965

American painters dominated the world's art scene in the 1950s with their pioneering work in the Abstract Expressionist style. Only a decade later, a new wave of U.S. artists began working in a less intellectual and more accessible style, painting celebrity icons, artifacts of everyday life and popular culture—including Lichtenstein's oversized paintings inspired by comic books. Upon his death in 1997, TIME hailed Lichtenstein's "cooled-out, impersonal style with a brightly colored, deadly fix on America's commercial culture."

Campbell's Soup 1
ANDY WARHOL
1964

Viewing the Pop Art scene of the '60s in the rear-view mirror, TIME declared, "No art movement in this century, American or European, has so quickly risen to influence and turned its inventors into moneyed stars." Warhol, the most famous of the group, acquired his fixation with ordinary products from the ground up: he spent the 1950s creating advertising art in New York City. Said TIME art critic Robert Hughes: "Warhol's fixation on repetition and glut emerged as the most powerful statement ever made by an American artist on the subject of a consumer economy."

Fission

BRIDGET RILEY

1963

Pop Art's fellow traveler in the world of '60s art was Op Art, in which artists explored optical phenomena that intrigued and fooled the eye, inducing in some a giddy, exhila-rating rush and in others a touch of seasickness. British artist Riley was a pioneer of the eye-candy style, whose playfulness, razzle-dazzle and emphasis on the experience evoked in the viewer are pure '60s. Her work, she said, celebrates "the pleasures of sight."

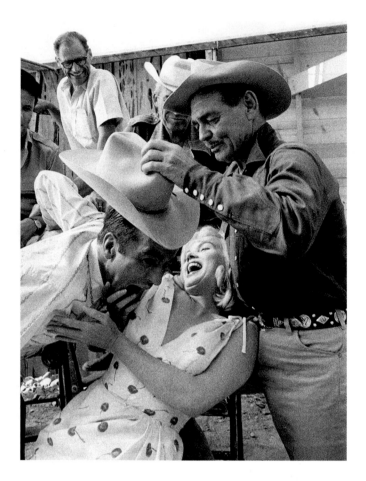

Marilyn Monroe and Clark Gable Filming *The Misfits*
BRUCE DAVIDSON
Reno, Nev. • 1960

Monroe's husband, playwright Arthur Miller, looks on as Montgomery Clift, left, horses around with Monroe and Gable on the set of *The Misfits*. Miller wrote the screenplay of the contemporary western as a vehicle for Monroe, whom he married in 1956, less than two years after her divorce from baseball star Joe DiMaggio. Levity was scarce on the difficult shoot; within 12 days of the end of production, Gable was dead and Monroe and Miller were separated. Monroe was fired from the film *Something's Got to Give* for erratic behavior in 1962, and she died from an overdose of barbiturates later that year, at 36.

Elizabeth Taylor and Richard Burton Filming *Who's Afraid of Virginia Woolf?*
UNKNOWN PHOTOGRAPHER
Hollywood • 1966

Director Mike Nichols stands beside the camera as the two stars film the scorching marital drama by Edward Albee. Taylor and Burton made headlines throughout the decade with their extravagant romance, which began on the set of the pricey but doomed costume drama *Cleopatra* (1963). The hard-drinking Welshman and the former child star both left their spouses to pursue their headlong love affair.

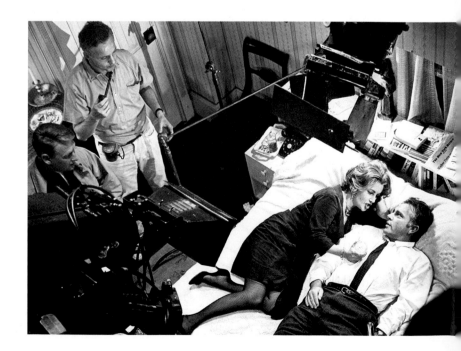

Julie Andrews Filming *The Sound of Music*

UNKNOWN PHOTOGRAPHER
Salzburg, Austria • 1964

Raised by two stage performers, Andrews was a British phenomenon in the 1950s; her clear soprano first stunned London audiences when she was only 12. She conquered Broadway as Eliza Doolittle in *My Fair Lady* in 1956, when she was 21, then reigned as Guinevere in *Camelot*. But Hollywood producers thought she lacked box-office clout, and veteran star Audrey Hepburn was chosen to play Eliza in the film version of *My Fair Lady* in 1964. Andrews had the last laugh, as she starred in two films that still resonate with audiences, Walt Disney's *Mary Poppins* (1964) and the 1965 classic *The Sound of Music*.

Julia Child in Her Kitchen in France
MARC RIBOUD
Plascassier, France • 1969

When TIME put "Our Lady of the Ladle" on its cover in 1966, the magazine included one of her most memorable quotes in the first paragraph of its story. "No matter if she breaks the rules. Her verve and insouciance will see her through. Even her failures and faux pas are classic. When a potato pancake falls on the worktable, she scoops it back into the pan, bats her big blue eyes at the camera and advises: 'Remember, you're all alone in the kitchen and no one can see you.'" Above, Child savors life in the kitchen of her summer home, La Pitchoune, in Provence.